T0365611

I Hate Sushi

By:
Harold Katinszky
&
Wesley Larcom

Xlibris Publishing

Concept
by
Harold Katinszky

Credits:

DREAMLAND BOOKS.

A New And Big Words Book.
New And Big Word: "Sushi"
Xlibris

To my niece and nephew Alysia and Gregory, as well as to children of all ages everywhere.

To contact the author: Harold Katinszky
e-mail: skystars@pacbell.net

To order additional copies of this book, contact:
Xlibris
844-714-8691
www.Xlibris.com
Orders@Xlibris.com

ISBN: Softcover   978-1-4134-9668-0
        Hardcover   978-1-4134-9669-7

Print information available on the last page

Rev. date: 08/05/2021

EXTRA SPECIAL THANKS

We would like to take this opportunity in order to express our sincerest and most heartfelt gratitude to Toni Cabatingan, without whose tireless efforts, the level of consistent high quality of our publications could not have been possible. Thanks for sticking it out over the course of the last few years.

DISCLAIMER

When I was a boy my father often scolded me for using the word hate. . . . . I hated it! As long as hatred, bigotry and small mindedness exist in the world, how can people of good intention and kindred spirit refuse to acknowledge the existence of such a negative emotion? It is not the concept of hate but the practice and propagation thereof which continues to pose a threat. Even the Holy Bible makes use of the term hate approximately 85 times. Please do not take our usage out of context.

Harold Katinszky

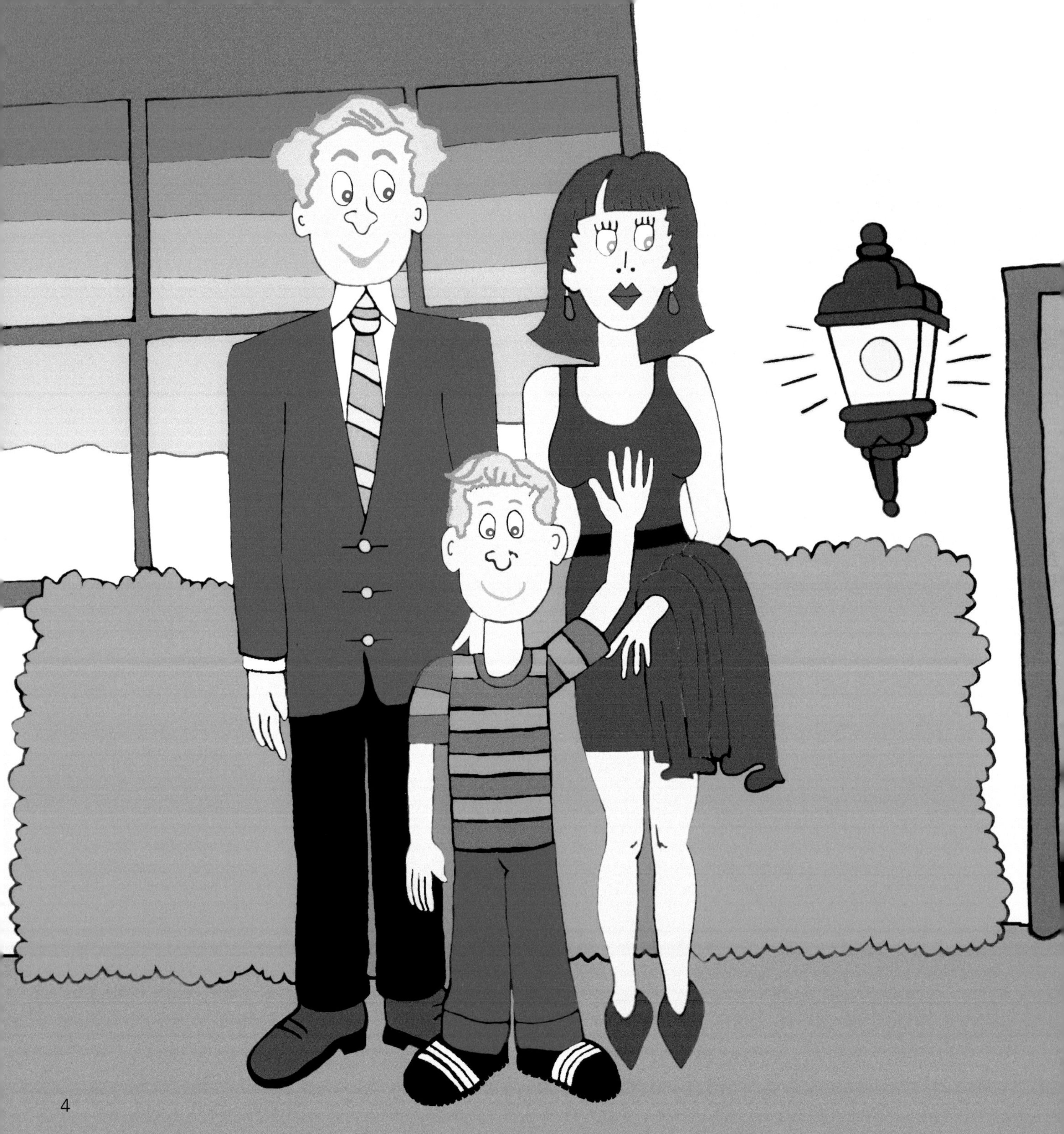

Hi, my name is Tommy. I live at home, with my daddy and mommy.

They are both great cooks, there is no doubt.
But once in awhile, for a treat we dine out.

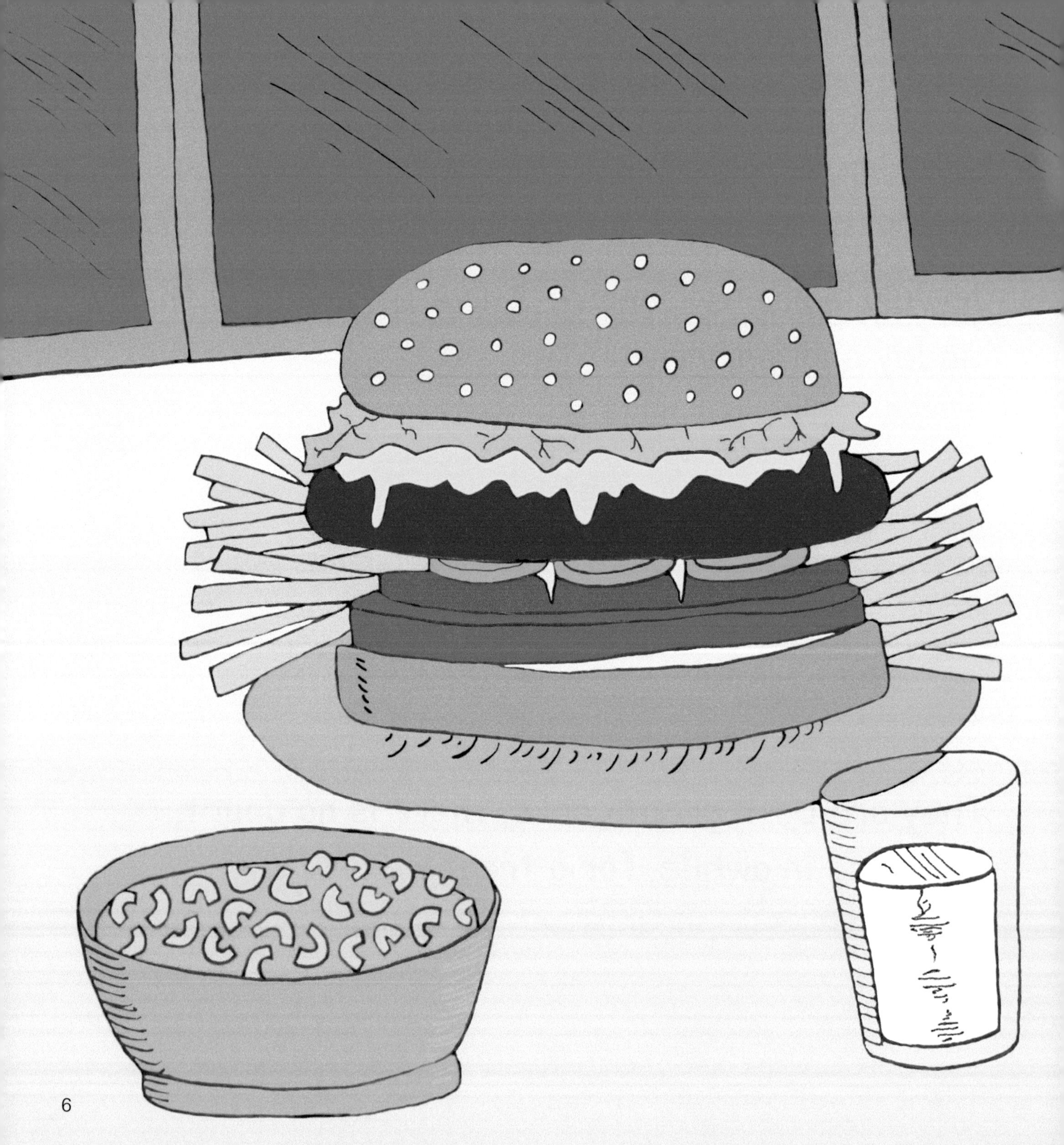

I like Macaroni, served with cheese, yet my favorite would be a Hamburger, with ketchup, if you please.

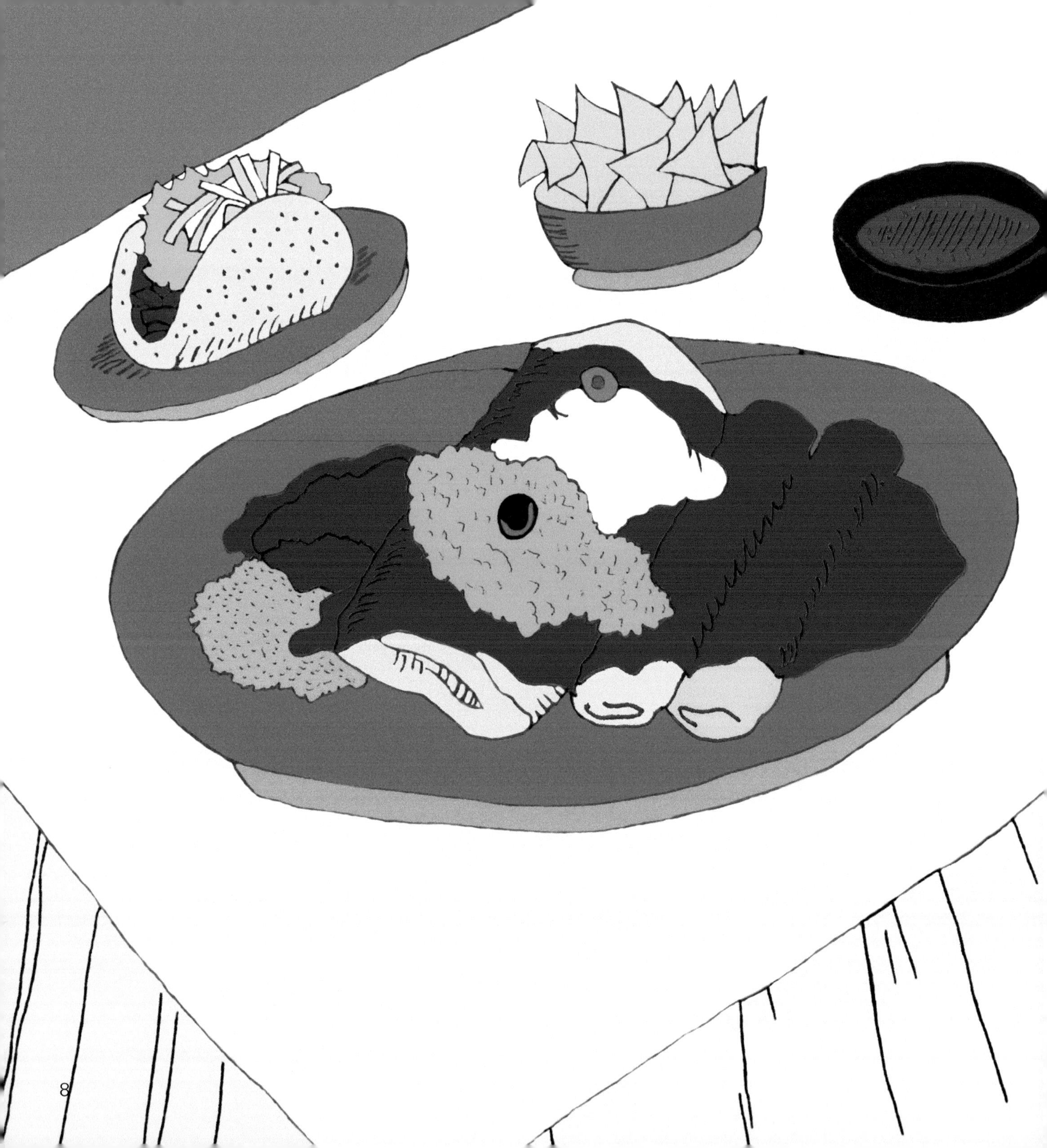

Sometimes we have Mexican when we go out to dine; I like Mexican food just fine.

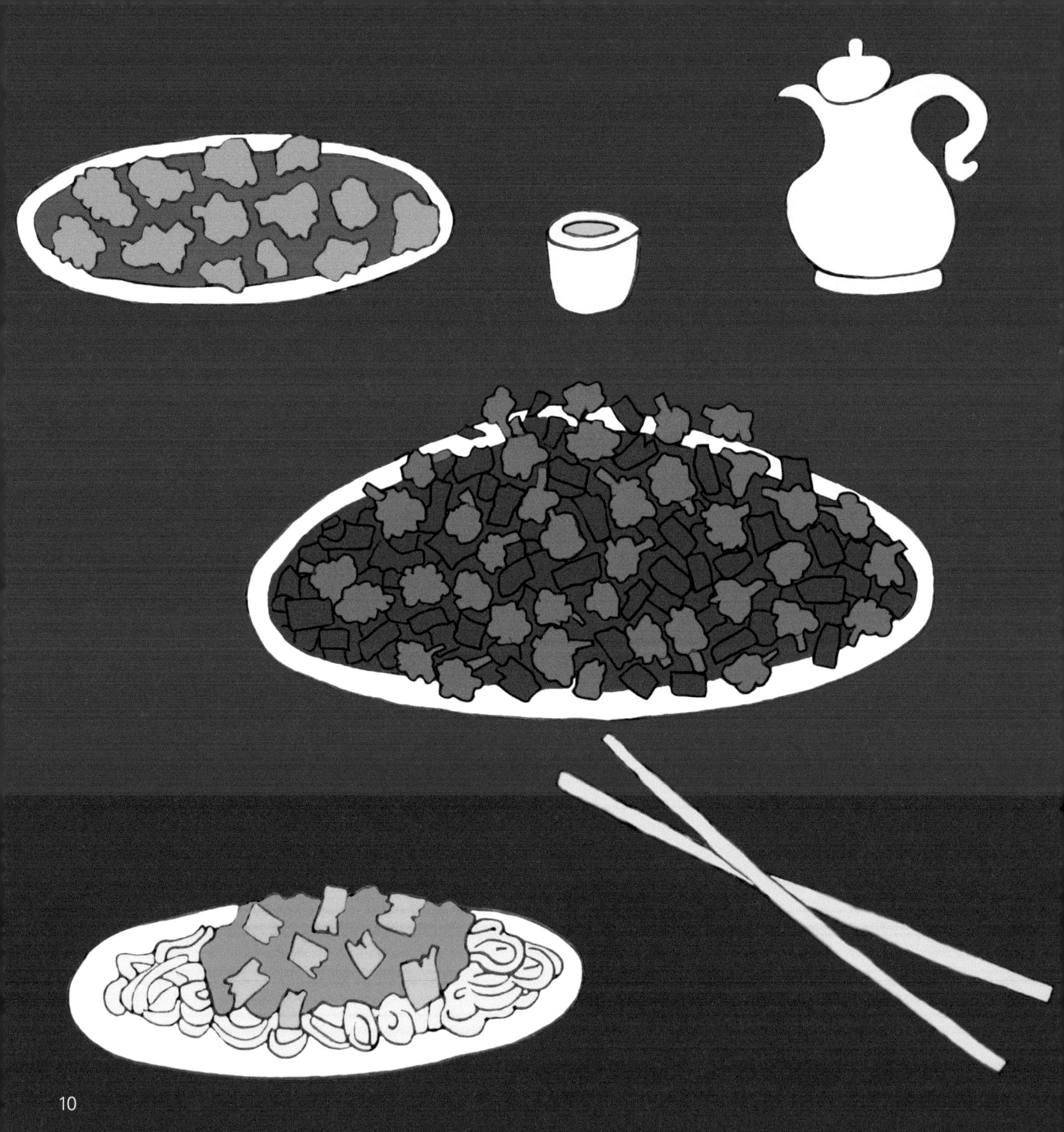

Chinese food is a favorite of mine, I'd eat Chinese anytime.

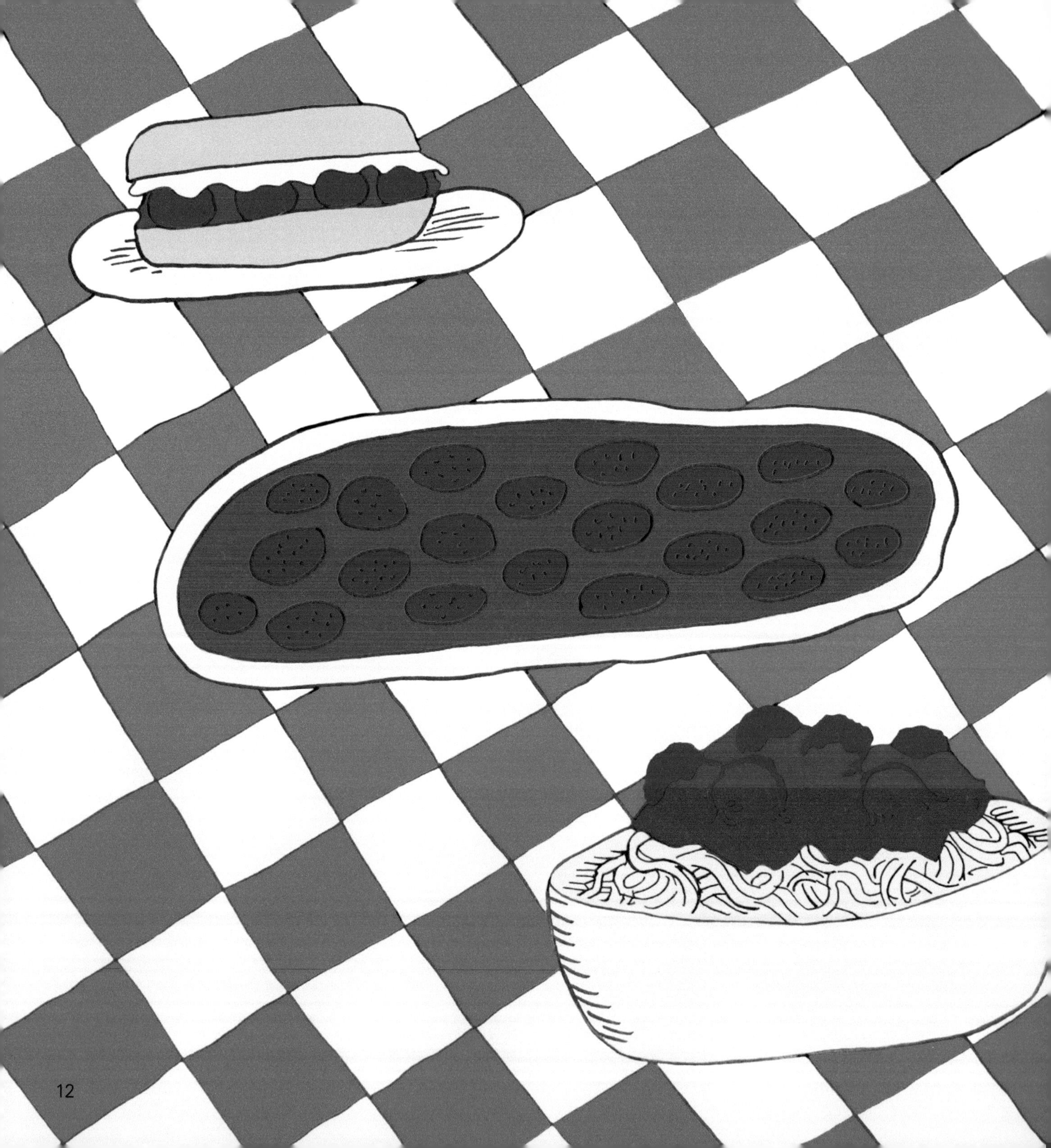

Sometimes, when I'm in the mood, I like to eat Italian food.

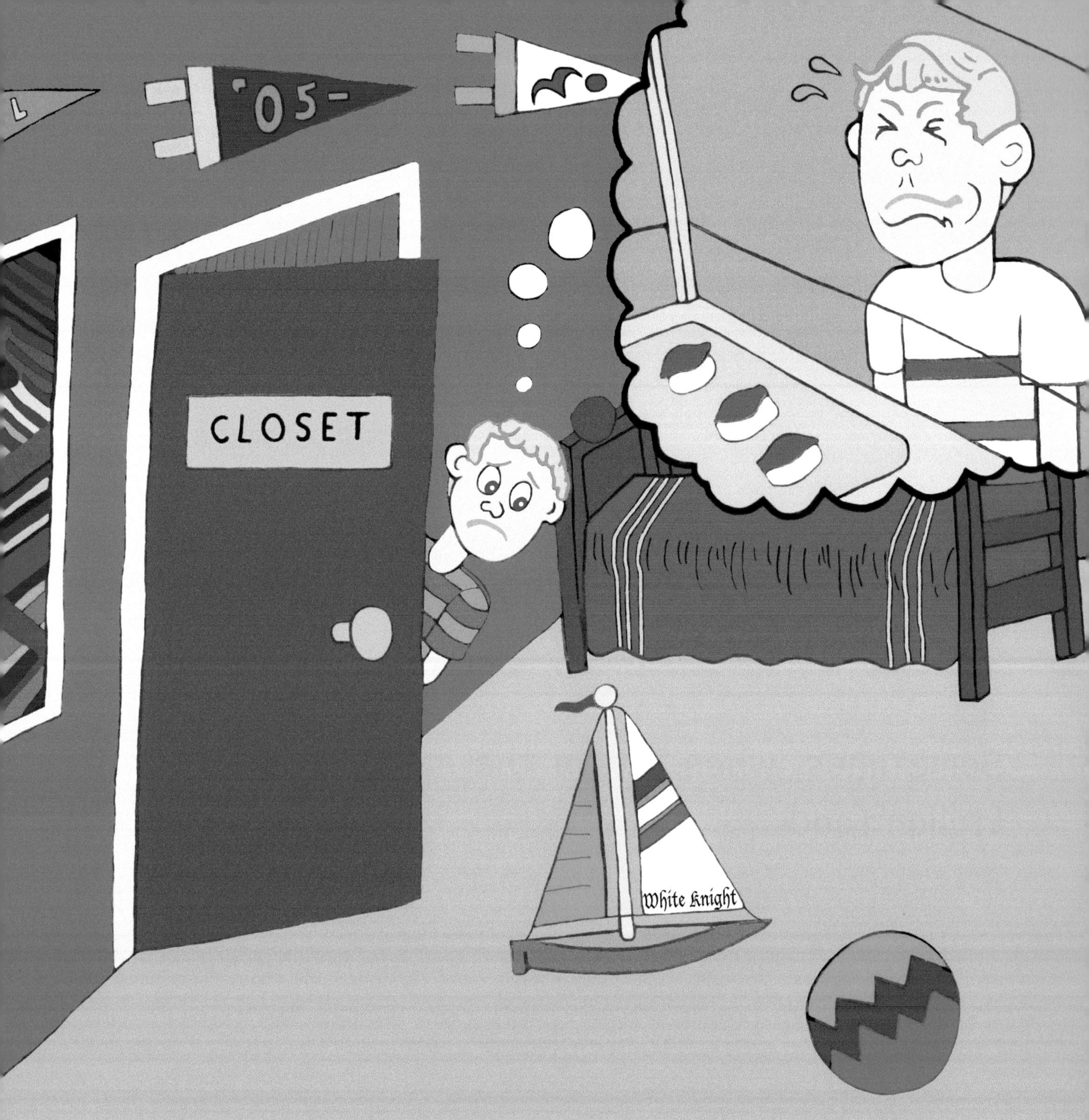
'05-
CLOSET
White Knight

Now I'm hiding, like a mouse. We're going to a restaurant called The Sushi House.

I once saw Sushi at the buffet; I don't like it-there's just no-way!

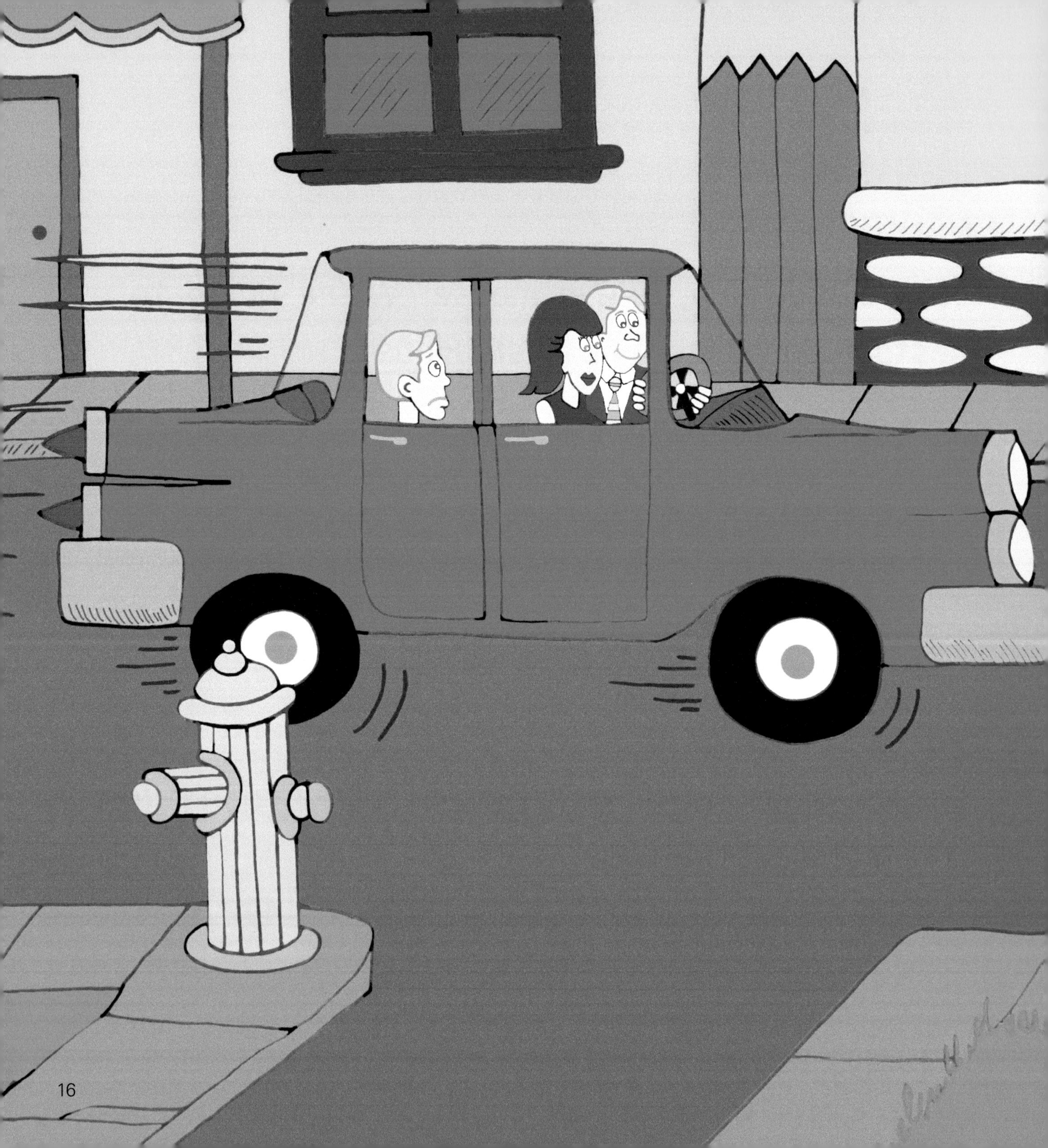

We're in the car and on our way. They won't listen to a word I say.

"I hate Sushi-it's not great. It looks like a ball of rice, with bait!"

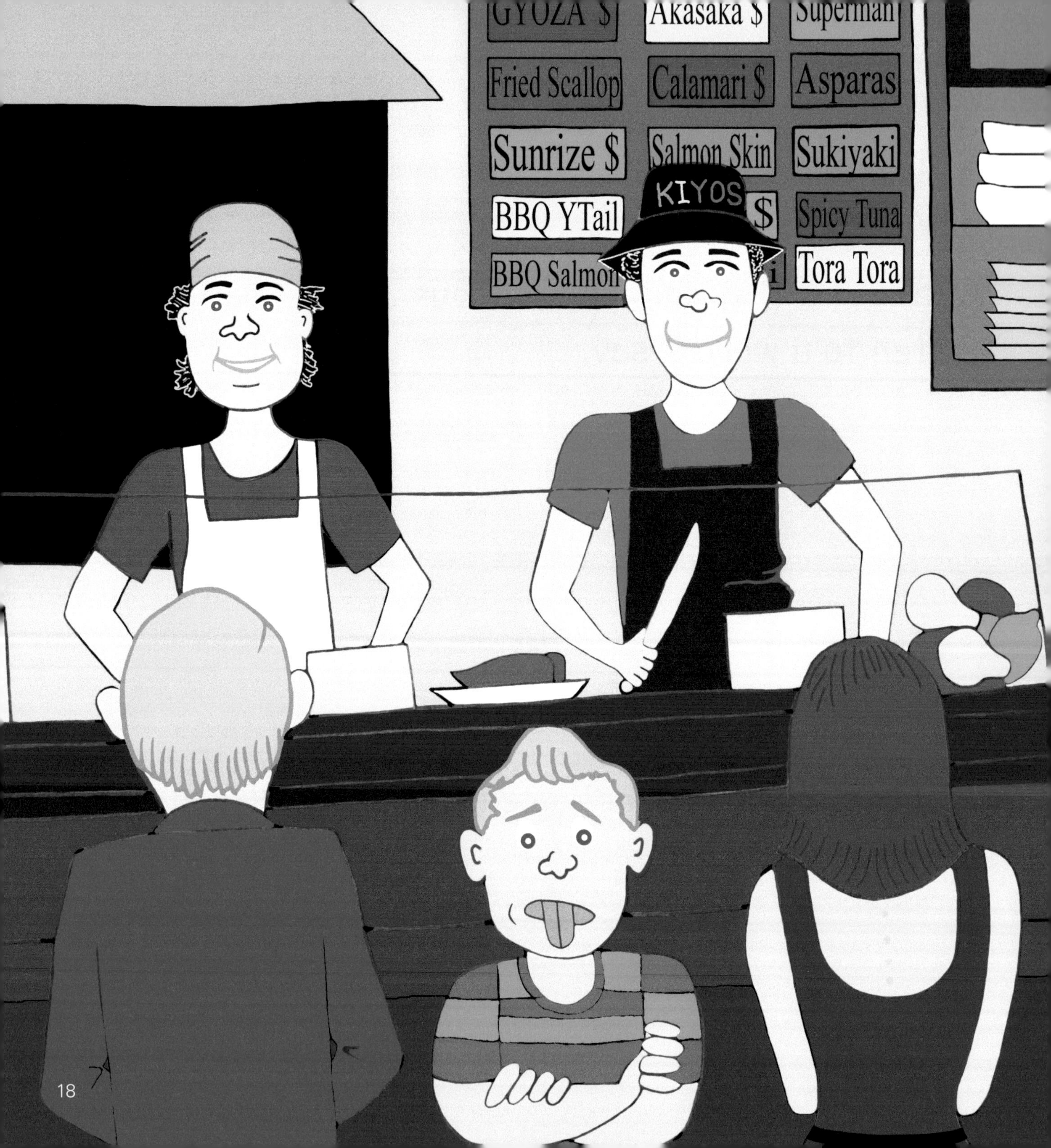
GYOZA $
Akasaka $
Superman
Fried Scallop
Calamari $
Asparas
Sunrize $
Salmon Skin
Sukiyaki
KIYOS
BBQ YTail
Spicy Tuna
BBQ Salmon
Tora Tora

Now we've arrived, dad's parked the car and we're seated at the Sushi bar.

With Yuki to the left and Kiyoshi on the right, they'll be our Sushi chef's tonight.

"I hate Sushi, it's not great, I do not want it on my plate!"

"Have some Sushi," say's Kiyoshi, "And you'll see, it's as delicious as can be."

"I hate Sushi-for the last time, keep it off this plate of mine!"

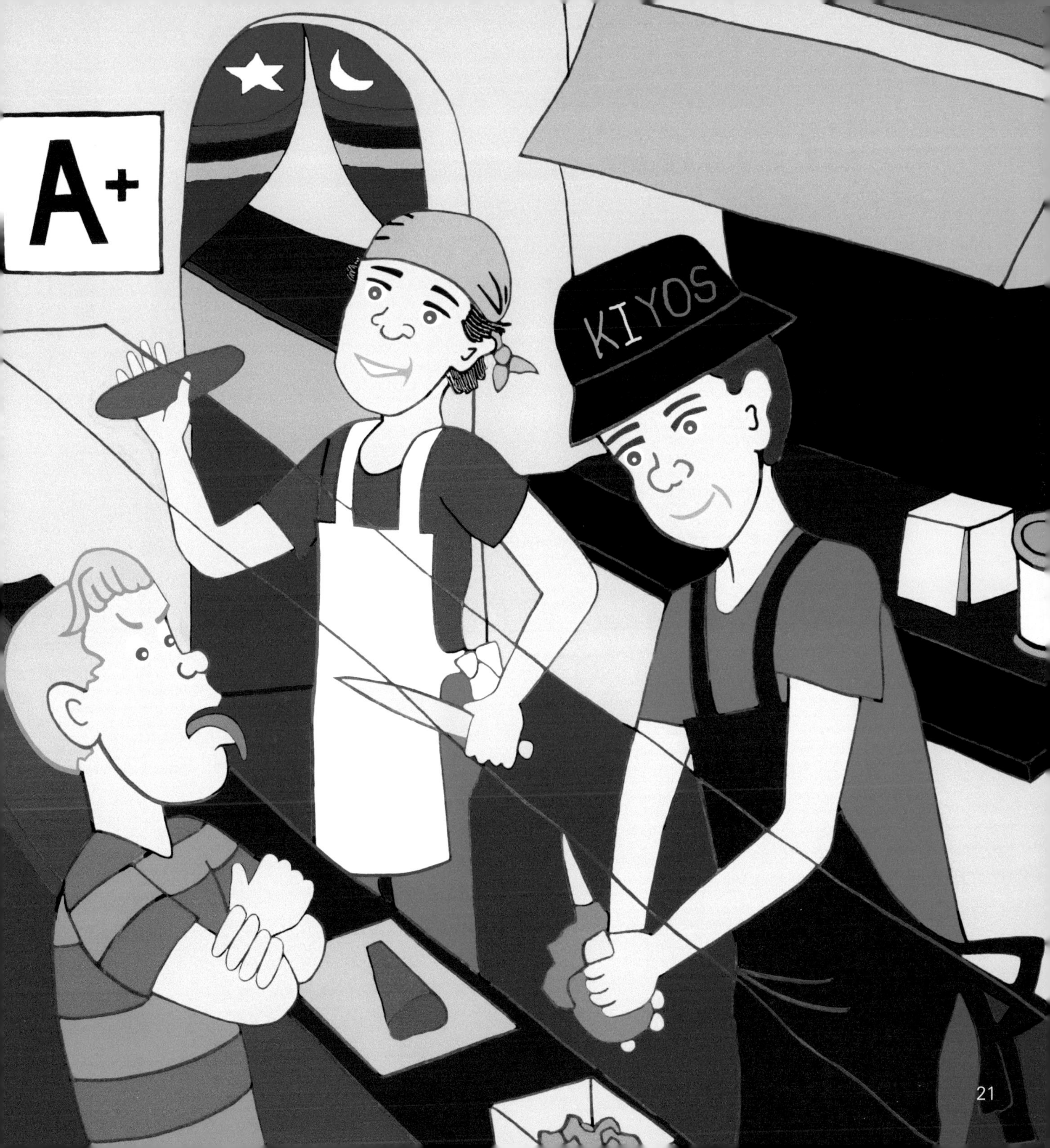
A+
KIYOS

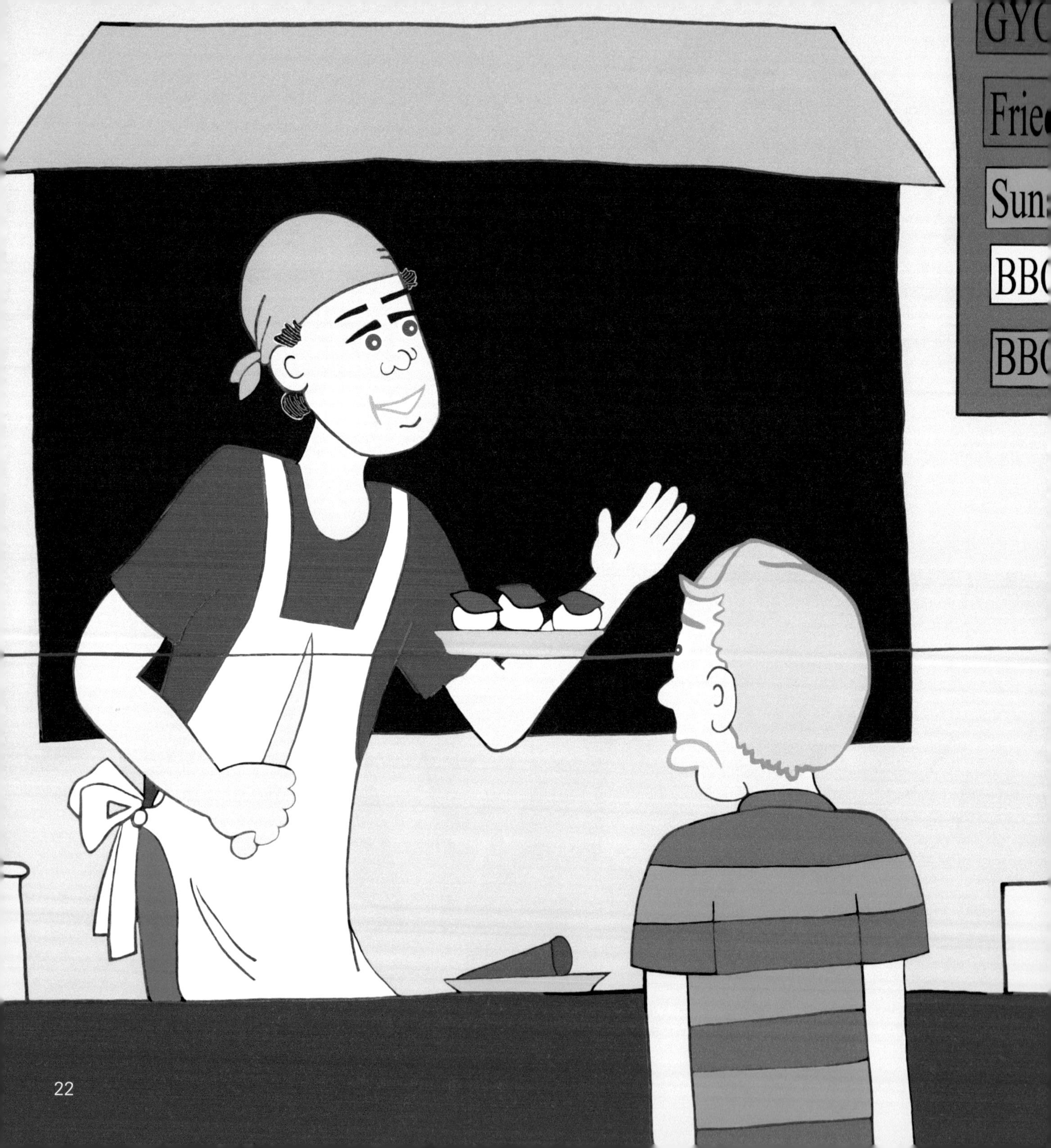

"Have some Sushi." Say's Yuki, "Kiyoshi is right, just wait and see."

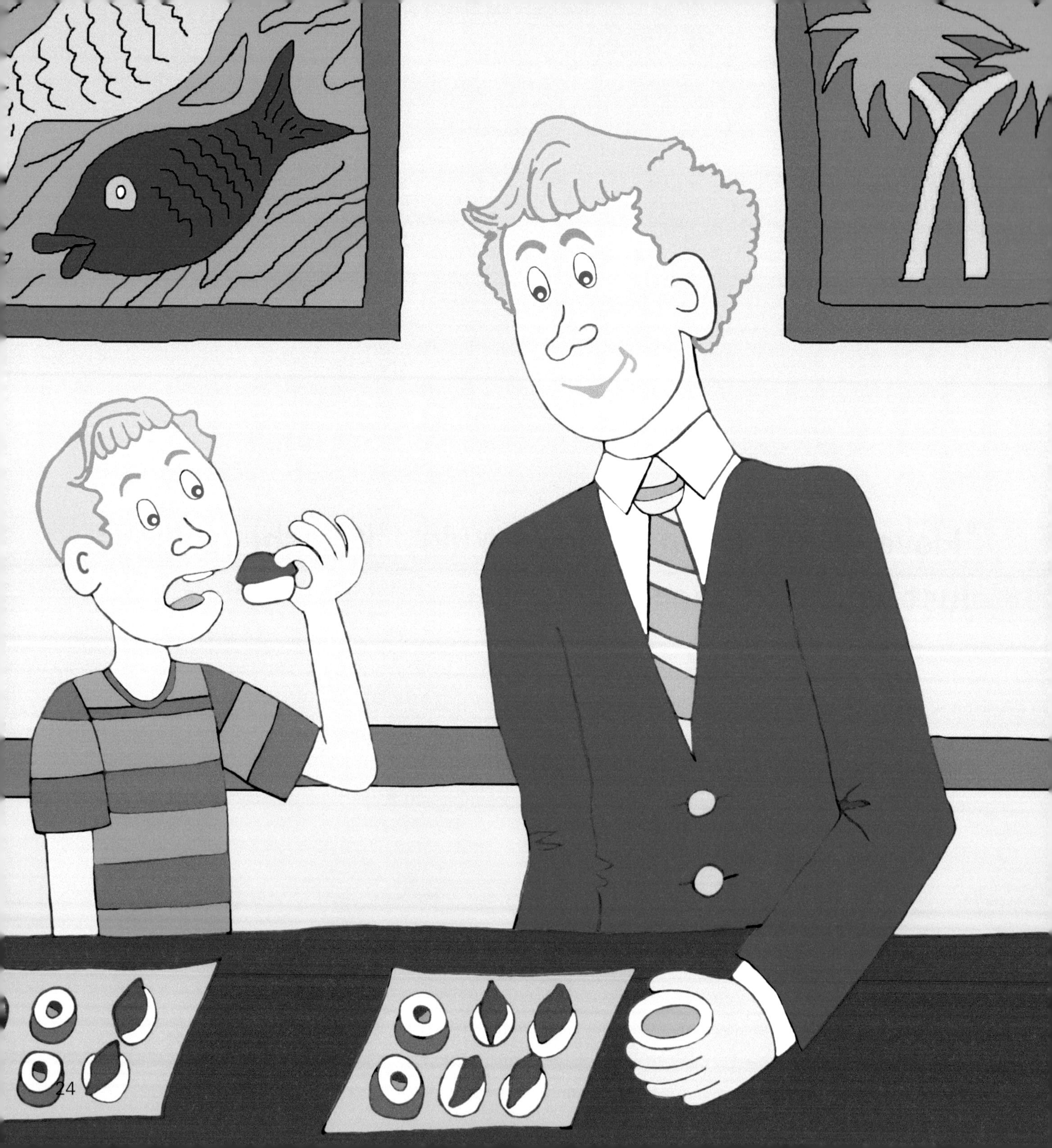

Dad says "Try some, you really should. Trying

new and different things is good."

Now mom and dad are most always right,
So I finally decide to take a bite.

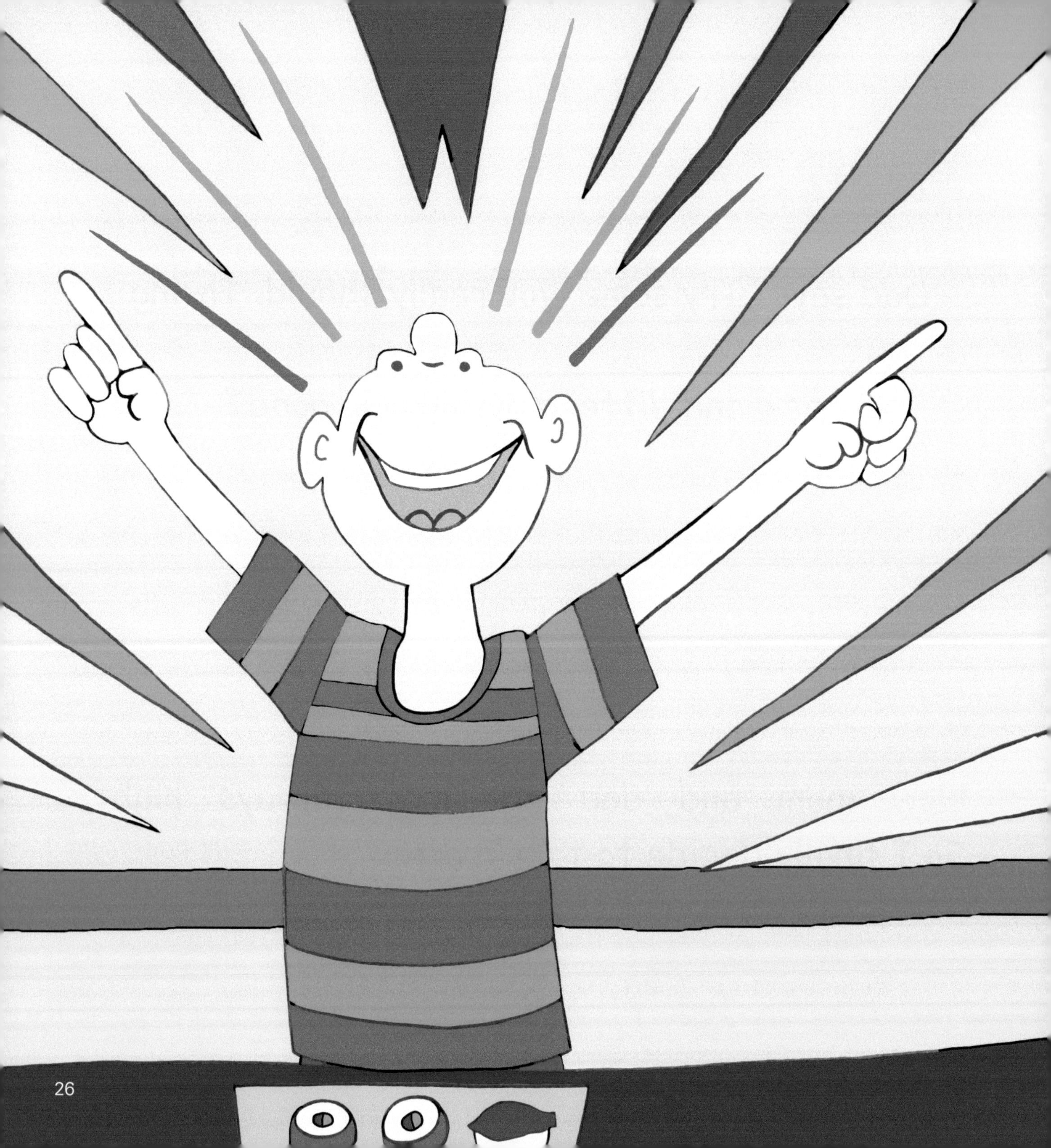

Hey! This Sushi is really good . . . . I like it, yes!

And never thought I would.

"I love Sushi, it tastes great! Please put some more upon my plate."

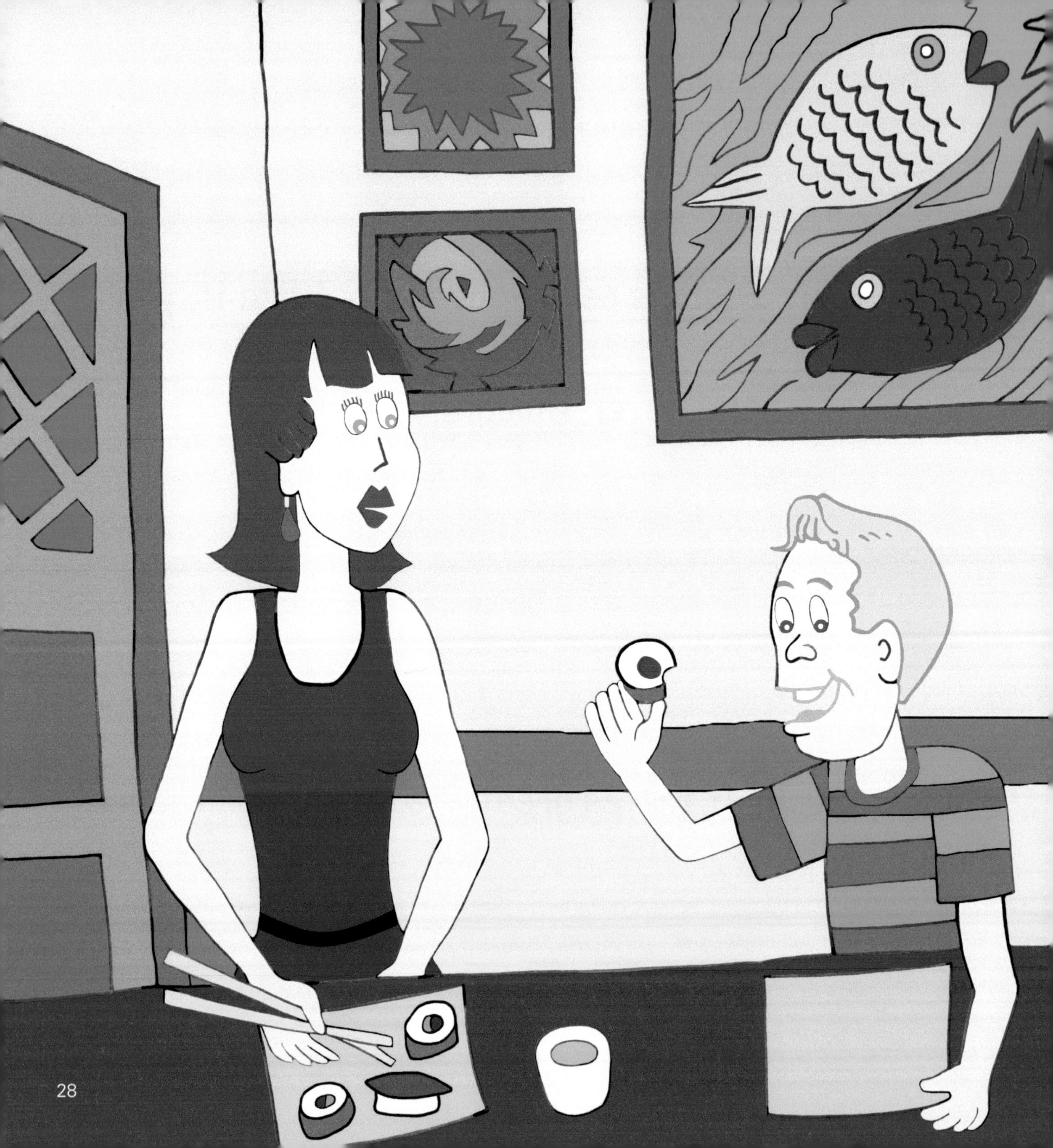

"See there?" Says Mom, "We told you, son. Trying new and different things is fun."

"Japanese food is really, really good. Would you like some more?" "Why, yes I would."

I eat and eat 'till I've had my fill, then it's time to pay the bill.

More reasonable than one might expect, Mom leaves a tip; Dad pays the check.

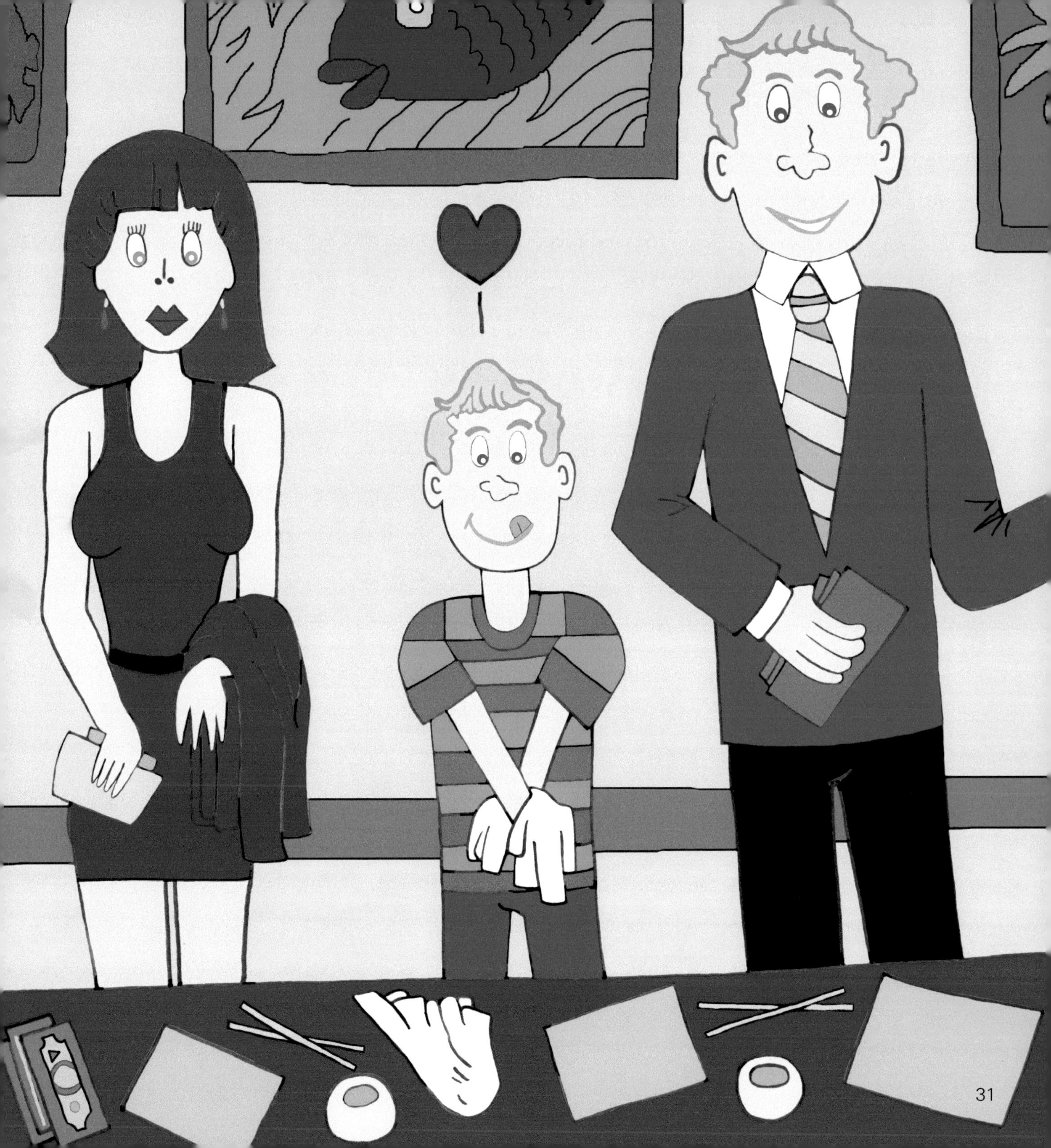

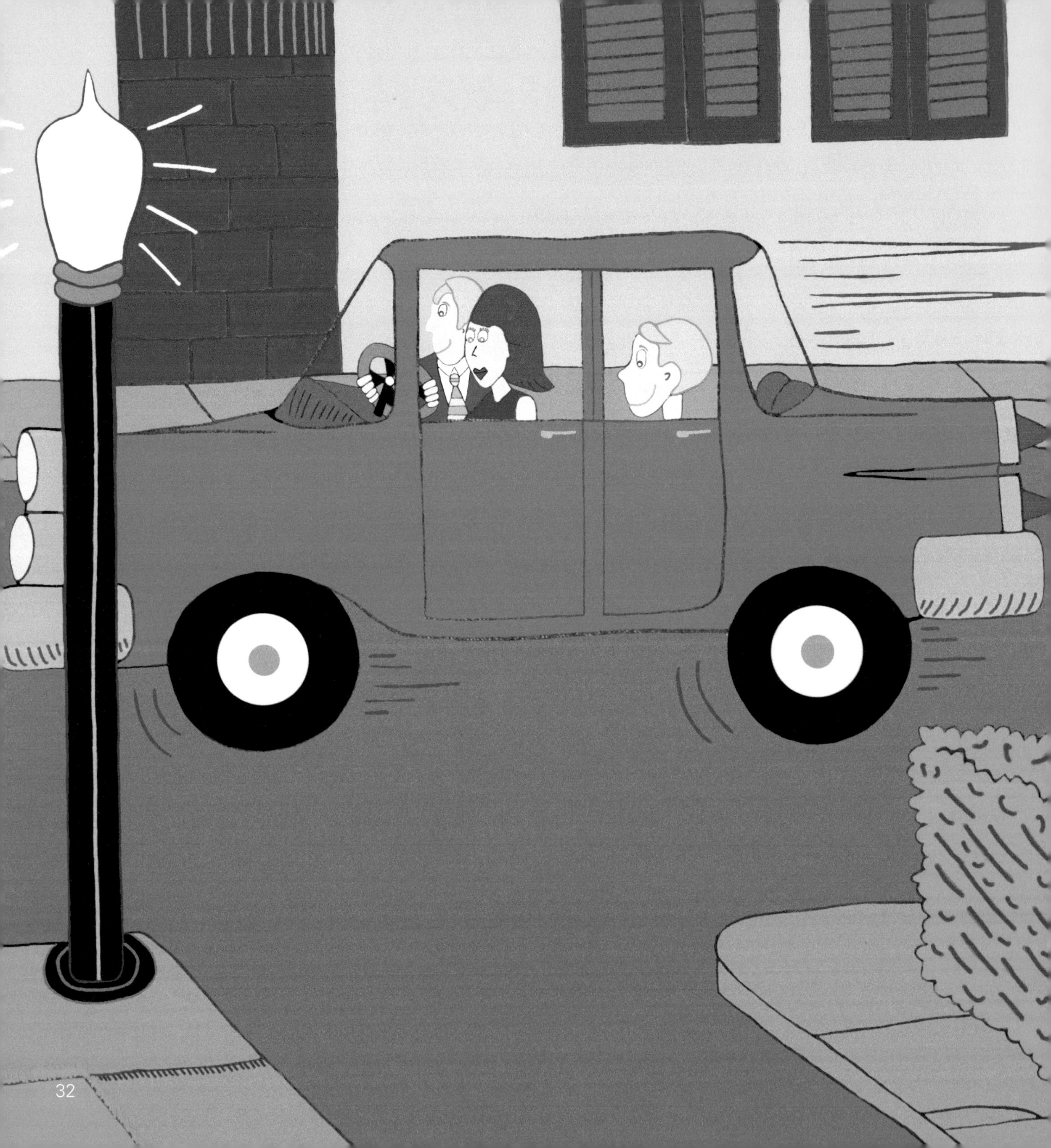

I love Sushi; it's really fine. I'd eat Sushi anytime.

Now we're all back in the car, on our way home from the Sushi bar.

You should give Sushi a try. Personally,

I love it,-goodbye.

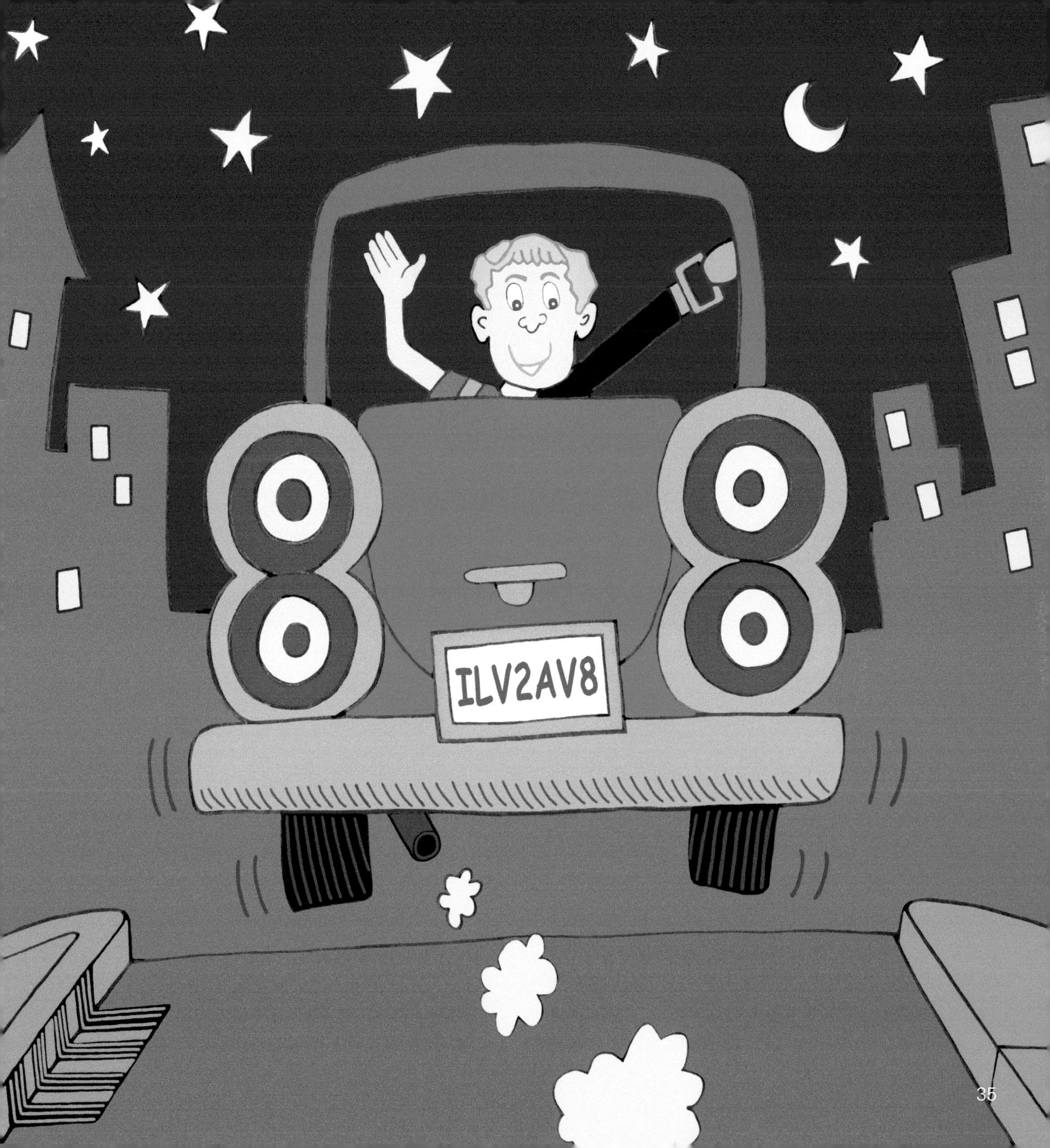
ILV2AV8

The End

Special thanks to:

Two celebrated world-class
Masters of Sushi

Kiyoshi & Yuki

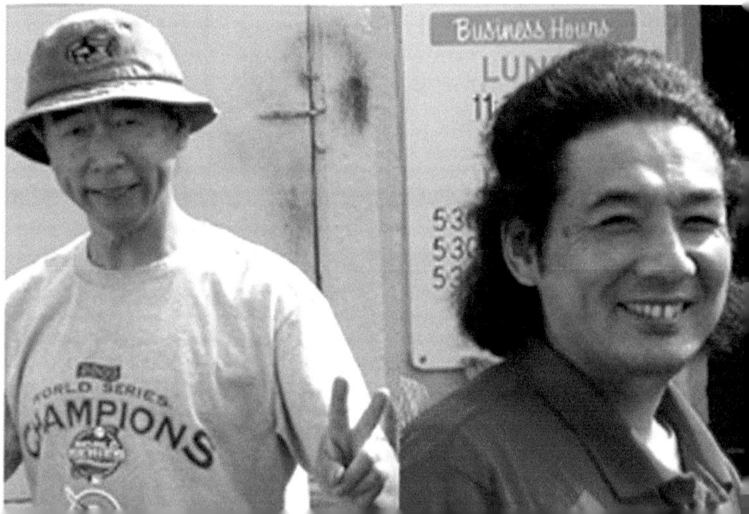
Business Hours
WORLD SERIES
CHAMPIONS

The Sushi House is Located on:

12013 West Pico Boulevard
Los Angeles, CA

Born and raised in California, Harold is a professional pilot and flight instructor with over 12,000 hours flying time in various aircraft. While he has thousands of hours in jets, he readily admits his favorite type of aviation outlet is soaring flight. Twice, he has flown and filmed our 50 states, extensively canvassing the United States from the air in motion pictures, encompassing nearly every major city and national landmark, as well as landing in all 50 states. www.Americabyair.com Harold creates in his art/film/recording studio with his longtime friend Wesley Larcom. Harold can be contacted at skystars@pacbell.net

Printed in the United States
by Baker & Taylor Publisher Services